50 Street Tacos You Can Make at Home

By: Kelly Johnson

Table of Contents

- Classic Beef Barbacoa Tacos
- Carnitas Tacos
- Grilled Chicken Tacos
- Al Pastor Tacos
- Fish Tacos with Lime Crema
- Shrimp Tacos with Mango Salsa
- Steak Tacos with Avocado
- Ground Turkey Tacos
- Chorizo Tacos
- BBQ Pulled Pork Tacos
- Veggie Tacos with Roasted Cauliflower
- Tofu and Avocado Tacos
- Korean Beef Tacos
- Baja Fish Tacos
- Grilled Veggie Tacos
- Pibil Tacos
- Spicy Chicken Tacos
- Beef and Potato Tacos
- Spicy Shrimp Tacos
- Black Bean and Corn Tacos
- Grilled Salmon Tacos
- Sweet Potato and Black Bean Tacos
- Lamb Tacos with Tzatziki
- Buffalo Cauliflower Tacos
- Ground Beef and Bean Tacos
- Duck and Pineapple Tacos
- Grilled Pork Tacos with Cilantro
- Zesty Lamb Tacos
- Thai Pork Tacos
- Roasted Beet Tacos
- Fried Fish Tacos with Cabbage Slaw
- Spicy Sausage Tacos
- Grilled Veggie and Hummus Tacos
- Grilled Steak with Chimichurri Tacos
- Chicken and Pineapple Tacos

- Spicy Beef and Jalapeño Tacos
- Fajita Chicken Tacos
- Eggplant and Quinoa Tacos
- Smoked Brisket Tacos
- Pork Belly Tacos with Pickled Onion
- Korean Pork Tacos
- Mahi Mahi Tacos
- Chipotle Chicken Tacos
- Bison Tacos
- Jackfruit Tacos
- Lamb and Feta Tacos
- Sweet Chili Shrimp Tacos
- Spicy Vegan Tempeh Tacos
- Bacon and Egg Breakfast Tacos
- Grilled Veggie and Pesto Tacos

Beef Barbacoa Tacos

Ingredients:

- 2 lbs beef chuck roast
- 1 onion, chopped
- 4 cloves garlic, minced
- 2 chipotle peppers in adobo sauce, chopped
- 1 tbsp cumin
- 1 tbsp oregano
- 1 tsp smoked paprika
- 1/2 cup beef broth
- Salt and pepper to taste
- Corn tortillas
- Cilantro, lime wedges, and onion for topping

Instructions:

1. Season the beef with cumin, oregano, paprika, salt, and pepper.
2. In a large pot, sear the beef on all sides. Remove the beef and set it aside.
3. Add onions and garlic to the pot, cooking until softened.
4. Add the chipotle peppers, beef broth, and beef back into the pot. Cover and slow cook for 6-8 hours until the beef is tender.
5. Shred the beef and serve on warm corn tortillas with cilantro, lime, and onions.

Carnitas Tacos

Ingredients:

- 2 lbs pork shoulder
- 1 onion, quartered
- 4 cloves garlic
- 1 orange, halved
- 1 tbsp cumin
- 1 tbsp oregano
- Salt and pepper to taste
- Corn tortillas
- Fresh cilantro, diced onions, and lime wedges for garnish

Instructions:

1. Rub the pork shoulder with cumin, oregano, salt, and pepper.
2. Place pork, onion, garlic, and orange in a slow cooker. Add water to cover.
3. Cook on low for 8 hours, then shred the pork.
4. For crispy carnitas, place shredded pork in a hot skillet and cook until crispy on the edges.
5. Serve in corn tortillas with cilantro, diced onions, and lime.

Grilled Chicken Tacos

Ingredients:

- 4 chicken breasts
- 2 tbsp olive oil
- 1 tbsp lime juice
- 1 tsp chili powder
- 1 tsp cumin
- Salt and pepper to taste
- Corn tortillas
- Shredded lettuce, avocado slices, and salsa for topping

Instructions:

1. Mix olive oil, lime juice, chili powder, cumin, salt, and pepper.
2. Coat the chicken with the marinade and refrigerate for at least 30 minutes.
3. Grill the chicken over medium heat for 6-8 minutes per side until fully cooked.
4. Slice the chicken and serve in warm tortillas with lettuce, avocado, and salsa.

Al Pastor Tacos

Ingredients:

- 1 lb pork tenderloin, sliced thin
- 1 tbsp achiote paste
- 1/4 cup pineapple juice
- 1/4 cup vinegar
- 1 tsp garlic powder
- 1 tsp onion powder
- 1/2 tsp chili powder
- Salt to taste
- Corn tortillas
- Pineapple slices, cilantro, and lime wedges for topping

Instructions:

1. Marinate the pork with achiote paste, pineapple juice, vinegar, garlic powder, onion powder, chili powder, and salt.
2. Let the pork marinate for at least 2 hours.
3. Cook the pork in a skillet over medium-high heat for 4-5 minutes per side.
4. Serve in tortillas with grilled pineapple, cilantro, and lime.

Fish Tacos with Lime Crema

Ingredients:

- 1 lb white fish fillets (like cod or tilapia)
- 1 tbsp olive oil
- 1 tsp paprika
- 1 tsp garlic powder
- Salt and pepper to taste
- 1/2 cup sour cream
- 1 tbsp lime juice
- Corn tortillas
- Shredded cabbage, avocado, and cilantro for topping

Instructions:

1. Season the fish fillets with olive oil, paprika, garlic powder, salt, and pepper.
2. Grill or pan-fry the fish for 3-4 minutes per side until cooked through.
3. Mix sour cream and lime juice to make the crema.
4. Serve the fish in tortillas with cabbage, avocado, cilantro, and lime crema.

Shrimp Tacos with Mango Salsa

Ingredients:

- 1 lb shrimp, peeled and deveined
- 1 tbsp olive oil
- 1 tsp chili powder
- Salt and pepper to taste
- 1 mango, diced
- 1/2 red onion, diced
- 1/4 cup cilantro, chopped
- 1 tbsp lime juice
- Corn tortillas

Instructions:

1. Toss shrimp with olive oil, chili powder, salt, and pepper.
2. Grill or sauté shrimp for 2-3 minutes per side until pink and cooked through.
3. Mix mango, red onion, cilantro, and lime juice to make the salsa.
4. Serve the shrimp in tortillas with mango salsa.

Steak Tacos with Avocado

Ingredients:

- 1 lb flank steak
- 1 tbsp olive oil
- 1 tsp cumin
- 1 tsp chili powder
- Salt and pepper to taste
- Corn tortillas
- Sliced avocado, cilantro, and lime for topping

Instructions:

1. Season the steak with olive oil, cumin, chili powder, salt, and pepper.
2. Grill the steak for 4-5 minutes per side, then let it rest for 5 minutes.
3. Slice the steak thinly and serve in tortillas with avocado, cilantro, and lime.

Ground Turkey Tacos

Ingredients:

- 1 lb ground turkey
- 1/2 onion, chopped
- 1 tbsp chili powder
- 1 tsp cumin
- 1 tsp paprika
- Salt and pepper to taste
- Corn tortillas
- Shredded lettuce, diced tomatoes, and cheese for topping

Instructions:

1. Cook the ground turkey with onions in a skillet until browned.
2. Add chili powder, cumin, paprika, salt, and pepper. Cook for another 2-3 minutes.
3. Serve the turkey mixture in tortillas with lettuce, tomatoes, and cheese.

Chorizo Tacos

Ingredients:

- 1 lb chorizo sausage, casing removed
- 1/2 onion, diced
- 1 clove garlic, minced
- Corn tortillas
- Fresh cilantro, lime wedges, and diced onions for topping

Instructions:

1. In a skillet, cook the chorizo over medium heat, breaking it apart as it cooks.
2. Add the onion and garlic, and cook until softened.
3. Serve the chorizo mixture in warm tortillas with cilantro, lime, and onions.

BBQ Pulled Pork Tacos

Ingredients:

- 2 lbs pork shoulder
- 1 onion, quartered
- 2 cloves garlic, minced
- 1 cup BBQ sauce
- Salt and pepper to taste
- Corn tortillas
- Coleslaw for topping

Instructions:

1. Season the pork with salt and pepper, and place it in a slow cooker with onion and garlic.
2. Cook on low for 6-8 hours until the pork is tender.
3. Shred the pork and mix with BBQ sauce.
4. Serve the pulled pork in tortillas topped with coleslaw.

Veggie Tacos with Roasted Cauliflower

Ingredients:

- 1 head cauliflower, cut into florets
- 1 tbsp olive oil
- 1 tsp cumin
- 1 tsp chili powder
- Salt and pepper to taste
- Corn tortillas
- Shredded lettuce, avocado, and salsa for topping

Instructions:

1. Toss the cauliflower florets with olive oil, cumin, chili powder, salt, and pepper.
2. Roast in a preheated oven at 400°F for 20-25 minutes, or until tender.
3. Serve the roasted cauliflower in tortillas with lettuce, avocado, and salsa.

Tofu and Avocado Tacos

Ingredients:

- 1 block firm tofu, drained and crumbled
- 1 tbsp olive oil
- 1 tsp cumin
- 1 tsp chili powder
- Salt and pepper to taste
- Corn tortillas
- Sliced avocado, cilantro, and lime wedges for topping

Instructions:

1. Sauté the crumbled tofu in olive oil with cumin, chili powder, salt, and pepper until golden and crispy.
2. Serve the tofu in tortillas with sliced avocado, cilantro, and lime.

Korean Beef Tacos

Ingredients:

- 1 lb ground beef
- 1 tbsp sesame oil
- 2 tbsp soy sauce
- 1 tbsp brown sugar
- 1 tbsp ginger, grated
- 1 clove garlic, minced
- Corn tortillas
- Sliced cucumber, shredded carrots, and cilantro for topping

Instructions:

1. Cook the ground beef in sesame oil until browned.
2. Add soy sauce, brown sugar, ginger, and garlic, and simmer for 5 minutes.
3. Serve the beef mixture in tortillas with cucumber, carrots, and cilantro.

Baja Fish Tacos

Ingredients:

- 1 lb white fish fillets (such as cod or tilapia)
- 1 tbsp olive oil
- 1 tsp chili powder
- 1 tsp cumin
- Salt and pepper to taste
- Corn tortillas
- Shredded cabbage, lime crema, and salsa for topping

Instructions:

1. Season the fish fillets with olive oil, chili powder, cumin, salt, and pepper.
2. Grill or pan-fry the fish for 3-4 minutes per side until cooked through.
3. Serve the fish in tortillas with shredded cabbage, lime crema, and salsa.

Grilled Veggie Tacos

Ingredients:

- 1 zucchini, sliced
- 1 bell pepper, sliced
- 1 onion, sliced
- 1 tbsp olive oil
- Salt and pepper to taste
- Corn tortillas
- Avocado, salsa, and cilantro for topping

Instructions:

1. Toss the zucchini, bell pepper, and onion with olive oil, salt, and pepper.
2. Grill the vegetables until tender and slightly charred, about 4-5 minutes per side.
3. Serve the grilled veggies in tortillas with avocado, salsa, and cilantro.

Pibil Tacos

Ingredients:

- 2 lbs pork shoulder
- 2 tbsp achiote paste
- 1/4 cup orange juice
- 1/4 cup lime juice
- 1 tsp cumin
- Salt and pepper to taste
- Corn tortillas
- Pickled red onions and cilantro for topping

Instructions:

1. Rub the pork shoulder with achiote paste, cumin, salt, and pepper.
2. Place the pork in a slow cooker with orange and lime juice.
3. Cook on low for 6-8 hours, then shred the pork.
4. Serve the pibil in tortillas with pickled red onions and cilantro.

Spicy Chicken Tacos

Ingredients:

- 1 lb chicken breasts
- 2 tbsp olive oil
- 1 tbsp hot sauce
- 1 tsp paprika
- 1 tsp garlic powder
- Salt and pepper to taste
- Corn tortillas
- Shredded lettuce, avocado, and cilantro for topping

Instructions:

1. Rub the chicken breasts with olive oil, hot sauce, paprika, garlic powder, salt, and pepper.
2. Grill or cook the chicken in a skillet for 6-8 minutes per side until fully cooked.
3. Slice the chicken and serve in tortillas with lettuce, avocado, and cilantro.

Beef and Potato Tacos

Ingredients:

- 1 lb ground beef
- 2 medium potatoes, diced
- 1 tbsp olive oil
- 1 tsp cumin
- 1 tsp chili powder
- Salt and pepper to taste
- Corn tortillas
- Shredded lettuce, diced tomatoes, and sour cream for topping

Instructions:

1. Cook the ground beef in olive oil until browned.
2. Add the diced potatoes and cook until tender, about 10-15 minutes.
3. Season with cumin, chili powder, salt, and pepper.
4. Serve the beef and potato mixture in tortillas with lettuce, tomatoes, and sour cream.

Spicy Shrimp Tacos

Ingredients:

- 1 lb shrimp, peeled and deveined
- 1 tbsp olive oil
- 1 tsp chili powder
- 1/2 tsp cayenne pepper
- 1/2 tsp paprika
- Salt and pepper to taste
- Corn tortillas
- Sliced avocado, cabbage slaw, and cilantro for topping

Instructions:

1. Toss the shrimp with olive oil, chili powder, cayenne pepper, paprika, salt, and pepper.
2. Cook the shrimp in a skillet over medium-high heat for 2-3 minutes per side until pink.
3. Serve the shrimp in tortillas with avocado, cabbage slaw, and cilantro.

Black Bean and Corn Tacos

Ingredients:

- 1 can black beans, drained and rinsed
- 1 cup corn kernels (fresh or frozen)
- 1 tbsp olive oil
- 1 tsp cumin
- 1 tsp chili powder
- Salt and pepper to taste
- Corn tortillas
- Avocado, salsa, and cilantro for topping

Instructions:

1. Sauté the black beans and corn in olive oil with cumin, chili powder, salt, and pepper for 5-7 minutes.
2. Serve the bean and corn mixture in tortillas with avocado, salsa, and cilantro.

Grilled Salmon Tacos

Ingredients:

- 1 lb salmon fillets
- 1 tbsp olive oil
- 1 tsp cumin
- 1 tsp paprika
- Salt and pepper to taste
- Corn tortillas
- Shredded cabbage, lime crema, and cilantro for topping

Instructions:

1. Season the salmon fillets with olive oil, cumin, paprika, salt, and pepper.
2. Grill the salmon for 4-5 minutes per side until cooked through.
3. Flake the salmon and serve in tortillas with shredded cabbage, lime crema, and cilantro.

Sweet Potato and Black Bean Tacos

Ingredients:

- 2 medium sweet potatoes, peeled and diced
- 1 can black beans, drained and rinsed
- 1 tbsp olive oil
- 1 tsp cumin
- 1 tsp chili powder
- Salt and pepper to taste
- Corn tortillas
- Avocado, salsa, and cilantro for topping

Instructions:

1. Roast the diced sweet potatoes in a preheated oven at 400°F for 20-25 minutes until tender.
2. In a skillet, cook the black beans with cumin, chili powder, salt, and pepper for 5 minutes.
3. Serve the sweet potatoes and black beans in tortillas with avocado, salsa, and cilantro.

Lamb Tacos with Tzatziki

Ingredients:

- 1 lb ground lamb
- 1 tbsp olive oil
- 1 tsp cumin
- 1 tsp garlic powder
- Salt and pepper to taste
- Corn tortillas
- Tzatziki sauce, cucumber, and mint for topping

Instructions:

1. Cook the ground lamb in olive oil with cumin, garlic powder, salt, and pepper until browned.
2. Serve the lamb in tortillas with a dollop of tzatziki, cucumber slices, and mint.

Buffalo Cauliflower Tacos

Ingredients:

- 1 head cauliflower, cut into florets
- 1 tbsp olive oil
- 1/2 cup buffalo sauce
- Salt and pepper to taste
- Corn tortillas
- Shredded lettuce, blue cheese, and celery for topping

Instructions:

1. Toss the cauliflower florets with olive oil, buffalo sauce, salt, and pepper.
2. Roast in a preheated oven at 400°F for 20-25 minutes until crispy.
3. Serve the buffalo cauliflower in tortillas with shredded lettuce, blue cheese, and celery.

Ground Beef and Bean Tacos

Ingredients:

- 1 lb ground beef
- 1 can black beans, drained and rinsed
- 1 tbsp olive oil
- 1 tsp cumin
- 1 tsp chili powder
- Salt and pepper to taste
- Corn tortillas
- Shredded cheese, lettuce, and salsa for topping

Instructions:

1. Cook the ground beef in olive oil until browned.
2. Add the black beans and season with cumin, chili powder, salt, and pepper.
3. Serve the beef and bean mixture in tortillas with shredded cheese, lettuce, and salsa.

Duck and Pineapple Tacos

Ingredients:

- 2 duck breasts
- 1 tbsp olive oil
- 1 tsp cumin
- 1/2 tsp cinnamon
- Salt and pepper to taste
- Corn tortillas
- Pineapple slices, cilantro, and lime wedges for topping

Instructions:

1. Season the duck breasts with olive oil, cumin, cinnamon, salt, and pepper.
2. Pan-sear the duck breasts for 4-5 minutes per side, then slice.
3. Serve the duck in tortillas with pineapple slices, cilantro, and lime wedges.

Grilled Pork Tacos with Cilantro

Ingredients:

- 1 lb pork tenderloin, grilled and sliced
- 1 tbsp olive oil
- 1 tsp cumin
- 1 tsp garlic powder
- Salt and pepper to taste
- Corn tortillas
- Fresh cilantro, lime wedges, and pickled onions for topping

Instructions:

1. Season the pork tenderloin with olive oil, cumin, garlic powder, salt, and pepper.
2. Grill the pork until cooked through, about 4-5 minutes per side.
3. Slice the pork and serve in tortillas with fresh cilantro, lime wedges, and pickled onions.

Zesty Lamb Tacos

Ingredients:

- 1 lb ground lamb
- 1 tbsp olive oil
- 1 tsp paprika
- 1 tsp cumin
- 1/2 tsp chili powder
- Salt and pepper to taste
- Corn tortillas
- Feta cheese, cucumber, and tzatziki sauce for topping

Instructions:

1. Cook the ground lamb in olive oil with paprika, cumin, chili powder, salt, and pepper until browned.
2. Serve the lamb in tortillas with feta cheese, cucumber, and tzatziki sauce.

Thai Pork Tacos

Ingredients:

- 1 lb pork shoulder, slow-cooked and shredded
- 1 tbsp soy sauce
- 1 tbsp fish sauce
- 1 tbsp lime juice
- 1 tsp ginger, grated
- Corn tortillas
- Shredded carrots, cilantro, and chopped peanuts for topping

Instructions:

1. Slow-cook the pork shoulder until tender and shred it with a fork.
2. Mix the shredded pork with soy sauce, fish sauce, lime juice, and grated ginger.
3. Serve the pork in tortillas with shredded carrots, cilantro, and chopped peanuts.

Roasted Beet Tacos

Ingredients:

- 2 medium beets, peeled and diced
- 1 tbsp olive oil
- 1 tsp cumin
- 1 tsp chili powder
- Salt and pepper to taste
- Corn tortillas
- Goat cheese, avocado, and arugula for topping

Instructions:

1. Roast the diced beets in a preheated oven at 400°F for 25-30 minutes, until tender.
2. Toss the beets with olive oil, cumin, chili powder, salt, and pepper.
3. Serve the roasted beets in tortillas with goat cheese, avocado, and arugula.

Fried Fish Tacos with Cabbage Slaw

Ingredients:

- 1 lb white fish fillets, battered and fried
- Corn tortillas
- Shredded cabbage
- 1 tbsp mayo
- 1 tbsp lime juice
- 1 tsp cumin
- Salt and pepper to taste
- Salsa for topping

Instructions:

1. Fry the battered fish fillets until crispy and golden.
2. Mix the shredded cabbage with mayo, lime juice, cumin, salt, and pepper to make the slaw.
3. Serve the fried fish in tortillas with cabbage slaw and salsa.

Spicy Sausage Tacos

Ingredients:

- 1 lb spicy sausage, cooked and crumbled
- 1 tbsp olive oil
- 1 tsp paprika
- Salt and pepper to taste
- Corn tortillas
- Sautéed onions, bell peppers, and hot sauce for topping

Instructions:

1. Cook the sausage in olive oil, breaking it apart into crumbles.
2. Season with paprika, salt, and pepper.
3. Serve the sausage in tortillas with sautéed onions, bell peppers, and hot sauce.

Grilled Veggie and Hummus Tacos

Ingredients:

- 1 zucchini, sliced
- 1 red bell pepper, sliced
- 1 red onion, sliced
- 1 tbsp olive oil
- Salt and pepper to taste
- Corn tortillas
- Hummus, arugula, and lemon wedges for topping

Instructions:

1. Grill the zucchini, bell pepper, and onion slices until tender and lightly charred.
2. Season with olive oil, salt, and pepper.
3. Serve the grilled veggies in tortillas with hummus, arugula, and lemon wedges.

Grilled Steak with Chimichurri Tacos

Ingredients:

- 1 lb flank steak, grilled and sliced
- 1 tbsp olive oil
- Salt and pepper to taste
- Corn tortillas
- Chimichurri sauce, diced onions, and cilantro for topping

Instructions:

1. Grill the flank steak to desired doneness, then slice thinly against the grain.
2. Serve the steak in tortillas with chimichurri sauce, diced onions, and cilantro.

Chicken and Pineapple Tacos

Ingredients:

- 1 lb chicken breast, grilled and sliced
- 1 cup pineapple, diced
- 1 tbsp olive oil
- 1 tsp chili powder
- Salt and pepper to taste
- Corn tortillas
- Fresh cilantro and lime wedges for topping

Instructions:

1. Grill the chicken breast and slice it thinly.
2. Toss the diced pineapple with olive oil, chili powder, salt, and pepper.
3. Serve the chicken and pineapple in tortillas with fresh cilantro and lime wedges.

Spicy Beef and Jalapeño Tacos

Ingredients:

- 1 lb ground beef
- 1 tbsp olive oil
- 1-2 jalapeños, sliced
- 1 tsp cumin
- 1 tsp chili powder
- Salt and pepper to taste
- Corn tortillas
- Sour cream, cilantro, and diced onions for topping

Instructions:

1. Cook the ground beef in olive oil, adding the jalapeños, cumin, chili powder, salt, and pepper.
2. Serve the beef in tortillas with sour cream, cilantro, and diced onions.

Fajita Chicken Tacos

Ingredients:

- 1 lb chicken breast, sliced
- 1 tbsp olive oil
- 1 tsp cumin
- 1 tsp paprika
- 1/2 tsp garlic powder
- Salt and pepper to taste
- Corn tortillas
- Sautéed bell peppers and onions for topping

Instructions:

1. Season the chicken with olive oil, cumin, paprika, garlic powder, salt, and pepper.
2. Cook the chicken in a skillet until browned and cooked through.
3. Serve the chicken in tortillas with sautéed bell peppers, onions, and any desired toppings.

Eggplant and Quinoa Tacos

Ingredients:

- 1 eggplant, diced
- 1 tbsp olive oil
- 1 tsp cumin
- 1 tsp chili powder
- Salt and pepper to taste
- 1 cup cooked quinoa
- Corn tortillas
- Avocado and fresh cilantro for topping

Instructions:

1. Roast the diced eggplant with olive oil, cumin, chili powder, salt, and pepper until tender.
2. Mix the roasted eggplant with cooked quinoa.
3. Serve the mixture in tortillas with avocado and fresh cilantro.

Smoked Brisket Tacos

Ingredients:

- 1 lb smoked brisket, shredded
- 1 tbsp BBQ sauce
- Corn tortillas
- Pickled onions and fresh cilantro for topping

Instructions:

1. Shred the smoked brisket and mix with BBQ sauce.
2. Serve the brisket in tortillas with pickled onions and fresh cilantro.

Pork Belly Tacos with Pickled Onion

Ingredients:

- 1 lb pork belly, cooked and sliced
- Corn tortillas
- Pickled red onions
- Cilantro and lime wedges for topping

Instructions:

1. Cook the pork belly until crispy and slice it thinly.
2. Serve the pork belly in tortillas with pickled red onions, cilantro, and lime wedges.

Korean Pork Tacos

Ingredients:

- 1 lb pork shoulder, slow-cooked and shredded
- 1 tbsp soy sauce
- 1 tbsp sesame oil
- 1 tbsp gochujang (Korean chili paste)
- Corn tortillas
- Kimchi, sesame seeds, and sliced green onions for topping

Instructions:

1. Slow-cook the pork shoulder and shred it.
2. Mix the shredded pork with soy sauce, sesame oil, and gochujang.
3. Serve the pork in tortillas with kimchi, sesame seeds, and sliced green onions.

Mahi Mahi Tacos

Ingredients:

- 1 lb mahi mahi fillets
- 1 tbsp olive oil
- 1 tsp cumin
- 1 tsp chili powder
- Salt and pepper to taste
- Corn tortillas
- Cabbage slaw, avocado, and lime wedges for topping

Instructions:

1. Season the mahi mahi fillets with olive oil, cumin, chili powder, salt, and pepper.
2. Grill or pan-fry the fish until cooked through, then flake it into pieces.
3. Serve the mahi mahi in tortillas with cabbage slaw, avocado, and lime wedges.

Chipotle Chicken Tacos

Ingredients:

- 1 lb chicken breast, grilled and sliced
- 1 tbsp chipotle sauce or adobo sauce
- Corn tortillas
- Shredded lettuce, sour cream, and diced tomatoes for topping

Instructions:

1. Grill the chicken breast and slice it thinly.
2. Toss the chicken with chipotle sauce or adobo sauce.
3. Serve the chicken in tortillas with shredded lettuce, sour cream, and diced tomatoes.

Bison Tacos

Ingredients:

- 1 lb ground bison
- 1 tbsp olive oil
- 1 tsp cumin
- 1 tsp chili powder
- Salt and pepper to taste
- Corn tortillas
- Diced tomatoes, fresh cilantro, and sour cream for topping

Instructions:

1. Cook the ground bison in olive oil, adding cumin, chili powder, salt, and pepper.
2. Serve the bison in tortillas with diced tomatoes, fresh cilantro, and sour cream.

Jackfruit Tacos

Ingredients:

- 1 can young green jackfruit, drained and shredded
- 1 tbsp olive oil
- 1 tsp cumin
- 1 tsp smoked paprika
- Salt and pepper to taste
- Corn tortillas
- Avocado, lime, and cabbage slaw for topping

Instructions:

1. Sauté the shredded jackfruit with olive oil, cumin, smoked paprika, salt, and pepper until tender and slightly crispy.
2. Serve the jackfruit in tortillas with avocado, lime, and cabbage slaw.

Lamb and Feta Tacos

Ingredients:

- 1 lb ground lamb
- 1 tbsp olive oil
- 1 tsp garlic powder
- 1 tsp cumin
- Salt and pepper to taste
- Corn tortillas
- Crumbled feta cheese, fresh mint, and cucumber slices for topping

Instructions:

1. Cook the ground lamb in olive oil, adding garlic powder, cumin, salt, and pepper.
2. Serve the lamb in tortillas with crumbled feta, fresh mint, and cucumber slices.

Sweet Chili Shrimp Tacos

Ingredients:

- 1 lb shrimp, peeled and deveined
- 2 tbsp sweet chili sauce
- 1 tbsp olive oil
- Corn tortillas
- Shredded lettuce, diced mango, and cilantro for topping

Instructions:

1. Sauté the shrimp in olive oil and toss with sweet chili sauce.
2. Serve the shrimp in tortillas with shredded lettuce, diced mango, and cilantro.

Spicy Vegan Tempeh Tacos

Ingredients:

- 1 package tempeh, crumbled
- 1 tbsp olive oil
- 1 tsp chili powder
- 1 tsp paprika
- Salt and pepper to taste
- Corn tortillas
- Avocado, salsa, and cilantro for topping

Instructions:

1. Sauté the crumbled tempeh in olive oil with chili powder, paprika, salt, and pepper until crispy.
2. Serve the tempeh in tortillas with avocado, salsa, and cilantro.

Bacon and Egg Breakfast Tacos

Ingredients:

- 4 slices bacon
- 4 eggs
- 1 tbsp butter
- Corn tortillas
- Shredded cheese, salsa, and avocado for topping

Instructions:

1. Cook the bacon until crispy, then crumble.
2. Scramble the eggs in butter until cooked.
3. Serve the bacon and eggs in tortillas with shredded cheese, salsa, and avocado.

Grilled Veggie and Pesto Tacos

Ingredients:

- 1 zucchini, sliced
- 1 bell pepper, sliced
- 1 red onion, sliced
- 1 tbsp olive oil
- Salt and pepper to taste
- Corn tortillas
- Pesto sauce, arugula, and feta for topping

Instructions:

1. Grill the sliced vegetables, seasoning with olive oil, salt, and pepper, until tender.
2. Serve the veggies in tortillas with pesto sauce, arugula, and crumbled feta.

www.ingramcontent.com/pod-product-compliance
Lightning Source LLC
LaVergne TN
LVHW061956070526
838199LV00060B/4156